Regardless

31 Days of Prayer, Praise, and Thanksgiving

Regardless

31 Days of Prayer, Praise, and Thanksgiving

Michele C. Walker, Ph.D.

Living Well for Women, LLC
Publisher

Published by Living Well for Women, LLC
P.O. Box 3333
Crofton, Maryland 21114-3333
www.livingwellforwomen.com

Library of Congress Cataloging-in-Publication Data is on file at the Library of Congress, Washington, DC.

ISBN13:   978-1-7356263-0-7 (paperback)
ISBN: 978-1-7356263-1-4 (e-book)

About the Author

Michele C. Walker is a Christian writer, blogger, small group facilitator, clinician, adjunct professor, and professional coach. She's married to Derek and is the mother of two young men, Cameron Terrell and Blair Andrew. Michele feels deeply called to the inspirational, with a desire to see women become all that God has in mind as they traverse the mundane and extraordinary issues of life. It is her belief that every woman can deliberately live life well as she builds her spiritual acumen and forges forward despite inevitable challenges. With singleness of mind, Michele authors the weekly blog *Living Well for Women (www.livingwellforwomen.com)*. It's her way of sharing what she's learned about how God speaks to us in the midst of our daily realities.

Dedication

This devotional is dedicated to my mom, Veta, my aunt, Delores, and the memories of my nana, Marie, and my first small group leader, Evelyn. Each of these women has demonstrated well how a woman of faith can find daily joy in trusting God as she navigates through the challenges of life.

Acknowledgments

My life has been filled with the love of family and friends. There are simply too many to name them all. To my husband, Derek, thank you for your encouragement. To my sons, Cameron and Blair, thank you for teaching me how to be a better mother. Beverly Lucas, thank you for being the right coach at the right time! Rochelle Noel, thank you for your encouragement and assistance through this process. Monica Blanton-Lacy, thank you for your insights on the readings and for helping me organize this product. Evie Andrews and Karolyn Moss, thank you for sharing the *Living Well for Women* blog (www.livingwellforwomen.com) with the ladies of the church, and thank you to every woman who has shared how the weekly devotional has spoken to her specific need. Minister Cedric Brown, thank you for your very practical biblical insights to this writing journey and for your candor as a discipleship coach. I absolutely appreciate you! To the tribe I call my friends, I appreciate your consistent support and for asking me the hard questions. I love you much and thank God for you every day.

"What I want is for you to receive a well-earned reward because of your kindness."
(Philippians 4:16b)

Live well,

Michele

Table of Contents

Introduction

The way we choose to respond in difficulty exposes who we are. Some may believe that the issues we face shape the way we respond, but the truth is that our responses to challenges shape the way we think, feel, and live. We get to choose. When what's happening is out of our control, we can decide to wallow in self-pity, act out in a passive aggressive way, explode on others because of our internal anguish, shut down and become emotionally unavailable, or we can recognize the lesson in the event, change our course of action, regain our sense of self, and make a decision to live well *Regardless* of our circumstances.

We can choose to live well when we accept the truth of who we are and who God is. We can face our issues and frailties and simultaneously embrace the fact that God has a purpose and plan for everything that happens. We can live well *Regardless* of the way things are, and we can learn to fully embrace the promise expressed in Jeremiah 29:11 (NLT):

> *"For I know the plans I have for you," says the Lord. "They are plans for good and not for disaster, to give you a future and a hope."*

God has not forgotten that we're here or that we're living with mixed up emotions, among complicated people, with daunting tasks, and with depleted energy. He knows that we struggle to make clear decisions, desire to gain control over our finances, and question our parenting skills. He's ever aware that the years are passing, and we feel insecure about what we've done and have failed to do. He knows that we want more abundance in our lives but are uncertain about how and where to find purpose or if we've taken too long to begin our search. He knows.

One Sad Circumstance

2 Samuel 13 is a terrible story of lies, cruelty, disgust, violence, and isolation that hits us with the bricks of trauma. The passage tells the story of Tamar, King David's daughter, who falls prey to her half-brother's deception. With the crafty encouragement of his cousin Jonadab, the Bible tells us that Amnon feigns illness so that he can satisfy his long-harbored lust for his half-sister Tamar. In her innocence, Tamar would respond to her father's instructions to serve her half-brother by first preparing the soup that Amnon requested and then by feeding her brother with compassion. Tamar would be left alone with her male sibling with no paternal protection, with no witnesses, and with insufficient strength to fight off her half-brother's advances. Tamar's story is one of desperation, broken dreams, abandonment, and grief.

While the events of the story leave the reader feeling shocked, sympathetic, and maybe angry, there's a verse that dangles Tamar's life before us. 2 Samuel 13:20b says, "So Tamar lived as a desolate woman in Absalom's house." The use of the conjunction 'so' signals a point of decision and lets the reader know that a definitive result is coming. Before the offensive event occurred, Tamar likely hoped for a future of only good things, including the kind of life that was expected of the daughter of a king. After the attack, the trajectory of Tamar's life drastically changed and left her feeling lost, deprived, ravaged, and hopeless because she experienced trauma at the hands of her half-brother. 'So' she would exist under her brother Absalom's care.

What's the Point?

Why is this story even in the Bible? What good does it do us to know about a story of deception, violation, murder and defeat? The truth is that this story can inform our individual stories. Sometimes we learn great lessons from stories that turn out positively. At other times when we hear stories about unfavorable outcomes, we're more convinced than ever to avoid those kinds of decisions at all cost. I don't know about you, but I've lived long enough and have made enough of my own mistakes to glean truth and warning from another person's circumstance. I no longer need to test the 'fire' with my own finger. If I can avoid burning myself by learning from the experiences of others, I'm in!

Regardless can be defined in many ways:

- *Oxford Dictionaries* search of the word *Regardless* reveals the following definition:

  "without paying attention to the present situation; despite the prevailing circumstances"

- *Merriam-Webster* defines *Regardless* as:

  "in spite of difficulty, trouble, etc.; without being stopped by difficulty, trouble, etc."

- *Collins Dictionary* states:

  "If you say that someone did something regardless, you mean that they did it even though there were problems or factors that could have stopped them."

Regardless is a statement of "no matter what". It's a proclamation that whatever happens, we will not give in. We will relentlessly pursue our goal and continue the course. My Nana would often use the intensifier of the word by stating *"irregardless"*. In other words, 'Come what may, my eyes and thoughts are fixed and moving forward.'

As Christians, our *Regardless* must be willing to submit to Christ's instruction to live well, love well, and in so doing, honor Him well. Life circumstances happen. We take a more informed approach to what occurs when we make up our minds to surrender our processes and outcomes to the One who has our remedy. We don't have to give in to fear, heartbreak, exhaustion, disappointment, or opinions by making poor choices or by deciding to live defeated lives. We can experience these emotions yet avoid giving up.

John 16:33 is quite clear when Christ tells His disciples, "Here on earth you will have many trials and sorrows. But take heart because I have overcome the world." We can live abundantly right now despite our difficulties. We've been given a choice. We can drag our minds, emotions, and bodies through life, barely scratching the surface of our potentials, or we can lift our heads, embrace His truths, look our challenges in the eye and decide to live our best lives through the power of the Holy Spirit as we navigate through our life issues. Deuteronomy 30:19-20a (NLT) says:

> *Today I have given you the choice between life and death, between blessings and curses. I call on heaven and earth to witness the choice you make. Oh, that you would choose life, that you and your descendants might live! Choose to love the Lord your God and to obey him and commit yourself to him, for he is your life.*

There is a way to work to resolve financial difficulties and still be happy, to navigate family drama and maintain our peace, to respond to inconsistencies in our workplace and reflect Christ's standard, and to face health and wellness realities and develop a grateful heart. Life is made for living. We can make daily decisions about the quality of our lives, and those decisions lead to both intended and unintended results. So *Regardless* of what has happened to us, we can choose to view our circumstances as opportunities for change that honors God and blesses, influences, and draws others.

Yes, trauma is hard, and disappointments have the potential to set us back. It's not easy to wrap our heads around what's happening to us, but we have help. God gives each of us the gift and privilege of knowing who He is and of knowing ourselves better. After all, He's clearly telling us that He is our life and wants us to make the choice to live well.

Embracing a *Regardless* mindset is not about convincing ourselves that it's best not to attend to our issues, nor is it the search for the perfect life. Instead, it's learning to love ourselves well by taking good, consistent care of ourselves; managing our resources; discovering and using our skills and abilities; building vibrant relationships; playing with the kind of pleasure that refreshes us; giving from the abundance of our gratitude; and broadening our understanding of God's nature, love and plans for us. When it's all said and done, we can ask ourselves if we lived the way we were created to live. We don't have to live desolate lives, live below our calling, convince ourselves of wrong ideas, or become grumpy, lonely, isolated people. Instead, we can grow in our knowledge of God, challenge ourselves and others, pursue wholeness and peace, become complementary additions to the people in our world, and persevere despite what we face.

Living a *Regardless* life begins and ends with God. We have to build our spiritual muscles to live our everyday lives well. Since God responds to prayer, praise, and thanksgiving, we'll start there and trust Him for the results of our faithfulness.

As we take a little time to read each short devotion in this book, we'll sense God's presence and become more aware of what He's saying to us. This can lead us to reflect on what He's done or is doing in our lives and will hopefully draw us into a meaningful dialogue with Him each day. In time, and with effort, we will begin to discover the ways in which God has orchestrated events, sent help, opened doors, and protected us from ourselves, others, and circumstances.

Our journey needs to begin with prayer. Make a practice of talking with Him often every day. Let Him know what you've noticed about what He's doing. Allow those insights to lead you to acts of praise and thanksgiving. As you develop a heart of gratitude, what's happened to you won't be as significant as what He's doing in you.

God has given us everything we need to live well. With the gift we've been given, we can choose to live well *Regardless*!

Regardless

Instructions

Read. Pause. Reflect. Pray. Repeat.

- *Read each devotion with an open heart as God takes time to communicate with you.*

- *Take a moment to pause after each reading; allow yourself time to understand the message.*

- *Use the **Reflection** section to write notes about what you sense God is saying to you.*

- *Your reading may then generate a desire to pray for a personal need or desire. Use the **Prayer** section to write down your specific requests. When your prayer has been answered, go back to the specific prayer section and record the date that you received your answer. Doing this will provide you with encouragement to continue to trust God as you remind yourself of how He responded to previous requests.*

Whatever choice you make about the use of this devotional, my prayer is that it draws you into a deeper, more meaningful relationship with God and propels you into action as you learn to live well *Regardless!*

Regardless

DAY 1

Fathered

"Our Father, which art in Heaven ...."

Matthew 6: 9-13 (KJV)

A synonym for the word 'just' is 'simply'. There are times when the most appropriate thing to do, in the midst of whatever we're dealing with, is to 'just' pray. That's because God keeps it simple. He has given us a vehicle that allows us to become silent about our situations and vulnerable to Him. In return, He tells us everything we need to know. So, when we've embraced child-like faith, we are led to the Rock (Psalm 61:2) to simply pray. It is a *Regardless* frame of mind that keeps us close to our Source. No matter what we go through, we go to God.

Dear Father,

You are our Source. We control nothing and look to you for everything. We are filled with gratitude and thank you for being an ever-present, loving, and protecting God. Thank you for watching over us and for being our Guide.

You've called us to be reflective and vulnerable. You've asked us to let go of everything that holds us back and to allow you to work in our situations. Help us to be brave enough to listen to what you tell us about ourselves as you expose us to our own hearts and motives. Then, please forgive us for every time we've attempted to be our own god, tried to control our own situations, and pushed our will on others. Teach us what it means to be your child, with complete dependence on you each and every day. And we will give Your Name the Glory for who you are and for what you do.

In Jesus' Name we pray,

Amen

Reflection:

Prayer:

Regardless

DAY 2

Miraculous

At the customary time for offering the evening sacrifice, Elijah the prophet walked up to the altar and prayed, "O Lord, God of Abraham, Isaac, and Jacob, prove today that you are God in Israel and that I am your servant. Prove that I have done all this at your command. O Lord answer me! Answer me so these people will know that you, O Lord, are God and that you have brought them back to yourself."

1 King 18: 36-37 (NLT)

The fact that we know God, can speak to Him, and have the assurance that He's with us is a miracle. Think about it. Jesus decided to leave the comforts of Heaven to live among ordinary people. He taught, healed, and ate meals with everyday folks. Then he decided to die to give us access to his home and his company forever. That's just plain miraculous!

Elijah had the privilege of calling on God and commanding miracles that demonstrated God's sovereignty. There were so many other options, but Elijah chose God. He could have elected to blend in with the crowd of people who made contrary choices, but his eyes were fixed on his Creator. His obedience moved God to provide what he needed, and the people recognized God as Lord.

God may not send a flash of fire at our command, but He will respond to our cries when our hearts are turned in His direction. He has provided what we've needed with complete, open access. In His plan for creation, He even reserved a space within us for His presence and has made it impossible for anyone or thing else to rightly occupy that God-space. The resulting miracle becomes obvious when we recognize that we need Him, surrender our lives and circumstances to Him, develop a life of prayer, and decide to depend on and follow Him. For some, He is an insignificant intruder. For us, He is the God we can call on to meet every need we have and to draw us to Himself time and time again.

Prayer

   Lord, thank you for the privilege of knowing you and of being known by you. Help us to recognize the significance of your presence in our lives today.

In Jesus' Name,

Amen

Reflection:

Prayer:

Regardless

DAY 3

Just Pray

Are any among you suffering? They should keep praying about it. And those who have a reason to be thankful should continually sing praises to the Lord.

James 5:13 (NLT)

We have more than enough reasons to pray at all times. When we're stressed out, relaxed, annoyed, relieved, tired, or energized we need to connect with our Source. He provides a way station for every situation.

Prayer lifts. It opens our minds, provides focus, and changes our perspective. It's God's vehicle to connect, comfort, instruct, and interact with us. We resist it because we either want to live independent of His gifts and do our own thing, or we've convinced ourselves that we don't have time for it. Then our circumstances get our attention and we recognize its value again. But, when we choose to pray consistently, to draw close to Him and tell Him what's on our minds and in our hearts, we begin to see prayer as our first and best option.

God promises that our prayers are powerful (James 5:16), so why not exercise this benefit when all is well and use it when we feel weak. We can connect when we know what to do or when we need direction. We can talk to Him when we're awake in the middle of the night or when we're working during the day. *Regardless* of what's happening in our lives (or not) we're instructed to pray (1 Thessalonians 5:16). He has the emotional resources we need for every situation (even when we don't think we have a need) and will often surprise us as He responds to our faithfulness.

Prayer

    Lord, thank you for the gift of prayer. Help us to make a conscious decision to pray at all times and in all situations. Give us the words to say when we're speechless and interpret our hearts' true intentions as you respond to our needs.

                       In Jesus' Name,

                       Amen

Reflection:

Prayer:

Regardless

DAY 4

Yield

Since I know that it is all for Christ's good, I am quite content with my weaknesses and with insults, hardships, persecutions, and calamities. For when I am weak, then I am strong.

2 Corinthians 12:10 (NLT)

Our lives tend to be dynamic and sometimes a bit complicated. Drama finds us when we'd rather it leaves us alone. Family issues are always present, and we have to respond to any number of demands and tasks on any given day. In His sovereignty, God uses all these experiences to keep our knees bent in prayer.

In 2 Corinthians 12, Paul was dealing with some issue, a thorn, and he wanted relief—no, he begged for relief (v.8). Instead of releasing him from this burden, God would use this issue to move Paul to a position of prayer. Only prayer would expose Paul's true need and God's great power. When Paul prayed, he experienced renewal, drew closer to his Master, and was reminded of his absolute need for Him. Prayer kept Paul focused and moved his heart toward cooperation. His perspective about his burden changed, and he experienced peace despite his hardships and because of them.

Paul's story included pain first, prayer next, and then peace and contentment. As a result, he yearned to tell everyone about his inadequacies so that people would know his all-sufficient God.

Regardless

When we take our eyes off our difficulties and yield our hearts to our Father, He will provide a peace that surpasses all understanding (Philippians 4:7) and will strengthen us in the midst of our struggles. He tells us in Psalm 46:1 that He is "always ready to help in times of trouble". He's prepared to support, comfort, guide, and restore, but we must be willing to surrender. We have to decide to release control of whatever situation we're dealing with. When we are willing to be vulnerable, weak, dependent, surrendered, and faithful with a *Regardless* mindset, God's grace is present, and His provision is poured out on our behalf. In fact, He promises that if we allow ourselves to draw close to Him and obediently follow Him, we will reap the benefits of His insatiable blessings (Colossians 2:7).

It's the most unusual of formulas. God uses our distresses and hardships to demonstrate His loving kindness and tender mercies. He allows the storms in our lives to draw us closer to Him and to expose His character through us.

We win when we succumb. When we pray, we know God. When we yield to Him, we know peace.

Prayer

Lord, you know all that we deal with and all that we need. We release the need to control our situations and believe that you will respond with more than we could ever ask for or imagine.

In Jesus' Name,

Amen

Reflection:

Prayer:

Regardless

DAY 5

Don't Stop!

Always be joyful. Keep on praying. No matter what happens, always be thankful, for this is God's will for you who belong to Christ Jesus.

1 Thessalonians 5: 16-18 (NLT)

Nothing is more important than prayer. As a matter of fact, given our looming and expanding circumstances, we need prayer, prayer and even more prayer.

Let's face it, life happens every day. We're bombarded with news of what's going on and going wrong. We live among people who have a shifting moral compass and it can be difficult to be different. But we're challenged to understand what's happening, to be aware of our surroundings, and to discern and recognize what's right, holy, and God-honoring from what's temporary, debase, and in violation of what it means to be a Christian. We're called to stand out, to be distinct and peculiar (1 Peter 2:9), and to consider everything from a position of prayer.

We can live among the conflicted, be examples to the searching, and be blessed in the midst of our challenging circumstances when we choose to pray at all times. It's the best course of action.

Regardless of what is happening around us and within us, trusting God and following His instructions results in a good end. When we build a prayerful life, our acts of obedience reap the rewards of gratitude and joy.

So, let's pray, again.

Father in Heaven,

We are so grateful for all that you have done. You've been our Provider, Sustainer, Deliverer, and Friend. You've opened doors for us that seemed improbable, and you've met our unanticipated needs.

We've carried burdens that didn't belong to us, made decisions that were outside of your will, sought advice from unreliable sources, and avoided opportunities for Bible study and prayer. At times, we've gotten caught up in the mayhem that surrounds us, believed what's not true, said what we didn't mean, and forgot Whose we are. You've called us to be different. You've called us to prayer.

Please forgive us for the poor choices we've made. We want your will to be evident in every area of our lives. We submit our health, finances, family members, employment, recreation, and friends to you and trust that You will provide the instructions, resolutions, and peace we need to live the lives to which you have called us.

Thank you for the open invitation to draw near to You and for the assurance that you hear our prayers. Teach us to see humility as our most sacred option, to live well regardless of our circumstances, and to demonstrate the joy of the Lord to a world that needs to see our Savior.

In Jesus' Name,

Amen

Reflection:

Prayer:

Regardless

DAY 6

Now

When I pray, you answer me; you encourage me by giving me the strength I need.

Psalm 138:3 (NLT)

We pray because we recognize our own inabilities and weaknesses as compared to God's capable strength. Our assurance is that He hears and answers us. In fact, He responds immediately, even when we don't realize the nature of the response. His answer is the purest action we could ever hope for, being both sovereign and supportive.

When we believe that our prayer requests are unanswered, it's because our focus is so limited. His sovereign decision is to give us more than we ask for by providing inward support and the ability to endure trials, overcome fear, and wait for His Divine timing. In all of this, a thankful heart is realized.

In the Amplified Bible, our target verse states, "You made me bold and confident with (renewed) strength in my life." We need the courage that God provides because our life circumstances often leave us feeling spent and bewildered. Despite our weakness, He supplies what is needed to wait well.

Charles Albert Tindley, the son of a slave father and free mother, taught himself to read and write. In 1905, Rev. Tindley, dubbed one of the founding fathers of Gospel music in America, wrote these lyrics (Hymn Time, 2019):

Encourage my soul and let us journey on,
Though the night is dark and I am far from home,
Thanks be to God, the morning light appears.
The storm is passing over,
The storm is passing over,
The storm is passing over, Hallelu!

Prayer

Lord, thank you for the assurance that when we pray, you listen. Thank you for the invitation to converse with you about everything we have on our hearts. You provide a safe place for us to lay out all our issues and concerns. Teach us to pray first, pray often, and worry less.

In Jesus' Name,

Amen

Reflection:

Prayer:

Regardless

DAY 7

Call His Name

I bow before your holy Temple as I worship. I will give thanks to your name for your unfailing love and faithfulness because your promises are backed by all the honor of your name.

Psalm 138:2 (NLT)

What's in a name? When the name is Jehovah, it denotes sufficiency, sovereignty, truth, and might. God's name is holy and steeped in consistency. It's such a revered name that in Judaism it is not casually spoken or written.

We call His name in gratitude and in need. We say, "Jesus!" and the Holy Spirit goes to work to give that utterance from our lips true meaning. While our hearts may express "Help," "I need you," "I don't know what to do," "Tell me what to say," "Make a way for me," "I need relief," or "Thank you," God receives an outpouring of our hopes, dreams, intentions, and feelings. Our words are feeble, but His name has power.

We call on Him because He has protected us, provided for every need, given direction, and displayed His incomprehensible love toward us. He has been "an ever-present help in the time of need" (Psalm 46:10) and the only One we can consistently depend on. We can share our secrets with Him, and He will share His secrets with us (Psalm

25:14). When He makes a promise to us, He never breaks it because the very nature of His name requires it.

Our God, Jehovah, is worthy of our worship. We can call on His name with confidence and must handle His name with reverence and respect, recognizing its power to be and to do for His children what no one else can.

Prayer

Lord, you are everything we need: Father, Provider, Protector, and Friend. We use our feeble voices to bless you as our hearts overflow with thanksgiving. You have been a ready, on-time, responsive God. None compare to you. Your reputation stands perfectly in our minds. You've provided food and shelter, walked with us through one crisis after another, whispered in our ears to encourage us as we've prayed, and extended mercy that we could never purchase. Thank you for being our God, our Father, and our Lord.

In Jesus' Name,

Amen

Reflection:

Prayer:

Regardless

DAY 8

Express It!

O Lord, how long will you forget me? Forever? ... But I will trust in your unfailing love.

Psalm 13:1-5 (NLT)

Life isn't filled with rainbows and butterflies. We have real challenges to face and are occasionally distracted by our own thoughts and fears. We're not always able to see and speak honestly about our situations. The truth is that despite what we're experiencing, God is good.

In Psalm 13, David expressed his distress and frustration to the Lord. God wasn't moving fast enough for him. And by God's grace, the very act of talking it out and sharing how he felt, facilitated a change in perspective. As David gained renewed strength, his confidence and faith in God was restored. His countenance was lifted, his thoughts became clearer, and he was now prepared to wait for the Lord's timing regarding his problem.

Instead of nursing our wounds and engaging in destructive self-talk, let's go to the One who is "a very present help in the time of need" (Psalm 46:1). He will be our Encouragement, Provider and Sustainer. He will answer our prayers and meet our needs.

Prayer

Regardless

Lord, your Word tells us that you care about everything we face (Psalm 138:8). No request is too small, and no burden is too heavy. Listen to our prayers and hear what our hearts are unable to express. We want to see your way through difficult situations and know that you will provide the encouragement and direction we need.

In Jesus' Name,

Amen

Reflection:

Prayer:

Regardless

DAY 9

Persist

Then Rizpah, the mother of two of the men, spread sackcloth on a rock and stayed there the entire harvest season ....

2 Samuel 21:10

What does it mean to endure something, to stay put and remain there until the breakthrough comes? Rizpah's life was filled with indecencies and painful realities. As a concubine to King Saul, she became a pawn to seize the throne, and her two sons were executed and hung atop a mountain to appease a wronged nation. Her response was to remain with her dead sons, protecting their bodies day and night from vultures and wild animals from April to October. For six long months she swatted, poked, and shooed away predators from devouring the remains of her beloved children. Love fueled her efforts. She persevered despite grief, drought, animal attacks, night scares, hunger pangs, weariness, old age, and loneliness. Her faithfulness resulted in a decent burial, and then God sent the rain to end the famine.

There is no record that Rizpah sought help from God or man. She, instead, endured alone. Our challenges are likely less severe than hers, yet we struggle to continue in prayer and maintain our hope until our breakthrough arrives. We forget that we have the tools to manage our situations. We can cry out to God and continue in prayer day-after-day for the same issue with the assurance that He loves us, hears us, and will answer us, and send our help.

Rizpah's actions demonstrated love and faithfulness to her children, but our lives can demonstrate that in the midst of despair, difficulty, and drought, God will respond to us if we maintain a *Regardless* attitude and persist in prayer.

Prayer

Lord, teach us to embrace the words found in Psalm 88:1 to "cry out to you day and night," in the midst of our challenges, for your direction and your relief. And, we will remember to give You the praise ....

In Jesus' Name,

Amen

Reflection:

Prayer:

Regardless

DAY 10

Search

Search me [thoroughly], O God, and know my heart! Try me and know my thoughts! And see if there is any wicked or hurtful way in me and lead me in the way everlasting.

Psalm 139: 23-24 (Amplified Bible)

As Christians, we should be concerned about how others experience us. Are we kind? Gentle? Rough around the edges? Sarcastic? Unapproachable? It's an important issue. Each person may experience us very differently or may be exposed to multiple sides of our too complicated personalities.

We can demonstrate authentic love to others when we are more aware of how we make them feel. It's not a question of whether they like us, but rather it examines how well we demonstrate Christ during public and private interactions.

Christ's love provides us with a safe place to be exposed to ourselves and then make any needed changes. He can acquaint us with the issues, habits, preferences, fears, and pain that we have either avoided, ignored, or simply didn't realize were present. It's a journey for those who are committed to growth—the real life-long learners who want to leave a positive imprint on everyone around them. It's for those who desire that the time between their birth and death overflows with residual peace.

A prayer to "search me" gives us the opportunity to see what drives our core beliefs. God is interested in cleaning out the contaminants in our hearts that crowd out the good, wholesome experiences He has in store for us and for others around us. He doesn't want us to be a fragile, fragmented people who live without hope and promise, nor does He want us to treat others as poorly as we may treat ourselves.

Today, we can *live well* by asking the Father to expose our flaws to us and provide direction for change. We can be brave enough to accept what we see, and (with the power and direction of the Holy Spirit) make changes that last because He doesn't see us as an accumulation of faults. God sees us as "beloved" and "wonderful". Others should see that, too.

Prayer

Lord, we want to live honestly, aware of how we impact and influence the people we live, work, and play with. Thank you for loving us despite our faults and for the opportunity to make changes that honor You.

In Jesus' Name,

Amen

Reflection:

Prayer:

Regardless

DAY 11

Cry Out!

He does not ignore those who cry for help.

Psalm 9:12b (NLT)

We cry out, "Lord, help me!" and He comes to our rescue. We ask Him to change our circumstances, lighten our loads, hear our prayers, and be our Vindicator. We go to Him in prayer too long after grief has bent our backs, and He hears us. He waits for opportunities to demonstrate His loving kindness. Out of His wisdom, love, and compassion, He gives a well-resourced response to the cries of His children. He doesn't give us what we deserve. Instead, He gives us what we could never use currency to buy-- His tender mercies. When we trust Him, He brings us to an upright position, even through suffering, so that we can bear the load and become witnesses to those who need hope.

God's *racham*, or tender mercies, are beyond our comprehension. He longs to share His most precious reserves with us, to love on us, and to shelter and protect us. He is the God who extends His mercy, delivers His peace, and sends His justice. He renews our joy when we call out to Him—today, *Regardless*. So, cry out. Ask Him for help, for justice, and for strength to make it through another day. Petition Him to open and close doors, restore family finances, and bring children home. When the weight of the issues is on us, we have relief. Cry out!

Prayer

Lord, we need your help today more than we did yesterday. Hear our prayer, respond to our deepest need, and provide the kind of relief that restores and refreshes our souls.

In Jesus' Name,

Amen

Reflection:

Prayer:

Regardless

DAY 12

Look Up

"Then Elisha prayed, O Lord, open his eyes and let him see! The Lord opened his servant's eyes, and when he looked up, he saw that the hillside around Elisha was filled with horses and chariots of fire."

2 Kings 6:17 (NLT)

Fear is familiar. It's not unusual for us to fear things we can see and even fear things we imagine. We can build entire scenarios in our minds based on very little information and convince ourselves of things that aren't true. Sometimes we build these false realities out of ignorance. Other times, we nurse our wayward emotions with these unrelenting thoughts.

When he was surrounded by an opposing army that came to capture him, Elisha chose to pray. He didn't pray for himself. He prayed for his servant who was gripped with fear. The servant was afraid of how things looked and was unaware of the presence of other forces. When Elisha asked God to open his servant's eyes, the servant was able to see God's provision all around them.

Like Elisha, we are called to demonstrate faith rather than fear. As we face daily challenges, we can ask the Lord to open our eyes and allow us to see the truth of our situation. The truth is that He is with us despite the way things appear.

Let's not accept snappy sayings that aren't based on biblical truths. Fear is not a (positive) motivator. Fear steals joy. Since God has not given us that spirit (2 Timothy 1:7), we don't have to embrace it, reside in it, or choose it as our 'go to' emotion. We will feel fear. What we do with what we are feeling is a choice. We can feel fear and pray, feel fear and try something new, feel fear and change what we're doing, and feel fear and makeup our minds to move forward *Regardless*. If we choose to look up, we will see that what God is doing is greater than we'd ever imagined.

Prayer

Lord, it's so easy to forget that You know the future and are intimately acquainted with every circumstance that is headed our way. Since you know it all, and have a plan for every event, we can rely on you despite the way things appear. Thank you for giving us the blessed assurance that we serve a God who loves us, has a plan for our lives, and will walk with us through every situation. To live well, we have to give You our fears and press on ….

In Jesus' Name,

Amen

Reflection:

Prayer:

Regardless

DAY 13

Reflect

Yes, the Lord has done amazing things for us! What joy!

Psalm 126:3 (NLT)

Not every circumstance leads us to immediate expressions of joy. But when we take the time to reflect on God's goodness and to consider how things could have turned out, we should notice that He has indeed been good.

Reflection empowers us to continue our journeys and be present for others. When we were like Jonah and wanted to disobey the directions we were clearly given, God was relentless to steer us back on course (Jonah 3:1-3). When we found ourselves, like David, repenting, yet again, He was faithful to forgive (Psalm 51:1). When we didn't know how things were going to work out but attached ourselves to a faithful (woman of) God, as Ruth did, He responded in ways we could not have imagined (Ruth 4:13-15). And when our resources were challenged, and our faith wavered, He gave to us in abundance, just as He did for the widow who made bread of flour and oil for the prophet, Elijah (1 Kings 17:12-16).

God has protected us from known and unknown dangers, supplied our needs, and kept us in our 'right minds'. If it were not for His gracious hand, we certainly would have fallen into dire circumstances. What God has accomplished in, through, and for us is absolutely amazing. Never dependent upon our money, talent, or connections, God has demonstrated

His love, kindness and sufficiency when we were at our weakest points. While the world is spinning on a crazy axis, His love and care for us has flourished and His plan for us has remained consistent. What joy!

Prayer

    Lord, thank you for your consistent demonstrations of love. We see you everywhere and know that you will be with us in every situation.

In Jesus' Name,

Amen

Reflection:

Prayer:

Regardless

DAY 14

Release

"Don't worry about anything, but in everything, through prayer and petition with thanksgiving, let your requests be made known to God. And the peace of God, which surpasses every thought, will guard your hearts and minds in Christ Jesus."

Philippians 4:6-7 (HCSB)

An astute elementary school principal asked her seasoned staff to write a letter to their former selves on the event of their first day of work as professional educators. She wanted them to consider how their perspectives about the students and their own work had evolved. She asked them to reflect on the fears they'd harbored and take note of how exaggerated and irrational those fears had been. It was an opportunity to recognize that they'd grown past their initial worries and didn't need to be intimidated by the mystery of the task before them.

The verses in Philippians remind us to surrender to and give our concerns to God. The challenges in our lives are not greater than His capacity to act on our behalf. His track record is both good and consistent and His intent for the course of our lives has not changed.

Fear hinders our progress and distorts our perspectives. As our minds are finite, our ability to develop usable options are few. If we focus on what frightens us, we're doomed to embrace a limited mindset and questionable outcome.

When situations loom, it's time to be prayerful, to exercise gratitude, and to give God praise. Deliberately thank Him for whatever comes to mind, and keep thanking Him, *Regardless* of how you initially feel. Experience the lift that comes from focusing on how good God is and has always been. Recognize the significance of small things. Allow your heart and mind to embrace the peace that comes from God. Experience a refreshing sense of hope. Begin to look up! That's where our help comes from (Psalm 121:1).

Prayer

Lord, you have a response to every question we have and the best outcome to whatever we're dealing with. We surrender to You, today. We're releasing our worries and burdens so that we can clearly hear You speak to us, follow your direction, and observe your actions.

In Jesus' Name,

Amen

Reflection:

Prayer:

DAY 15

Relentless

Keep on asking, and you will be given what you ask for. Keep on looking, and you will find. Keep on knocking, and the door will be opened.

Matthew 7:7

There's no parent who tells his or her child to ask for something over and over again. It just doesn't happen. Children often wear parents out with their requests, occasionally adding a little whining, pleading, and 'nicey-nice' action to emphasize and realize their request. And, of course, once a child learns how to move a parent's response in their favor, it makes the task of getting future desires a bit easier.

God encourages us to be persistent in prayer. He wants us to ask again and again. As we engage, He teaches us how to pray the prayer that's good for us. He tells us what we didn't know, shows us what we couldn't see, and gives us what we couldn't ask for. Over time, we learn to pray in a way that lines up with His nature and we develop an openness of mind that anticipates a variety of Godly responses. We learn to release the choke hold on what we "must have" and trust what He will do.

Interestingly, Matthew 6 tells us not to worry (verse 25) and Matthew 7 tells us to keep on *asking, looking,* and *knocking*. Clearly, God builds our spiritual aptitude as we make our requests. We don't need to ask and worry, ask and complain, or ask and be cranky. We're instructed to "keep on ...." which undoubtedly means that we're to be unrelenting in making our requests. So, "keep on asking," and make the requests that He would make for us; "keep on looking," and search to understand who He is and what He prefers, and "keep on knocking," and stubbornly wait for opportunities to open widely.

God wants us to embrace a *Regardless* mindset and relentlessly pursue Him in prayer. His responses to that faithful act will teach us about Him and about ourselves.

Prayer

> *Lord, teach us how to pray the prayer that moves you and matures us.*

> *In Jesus' Name,*

> *Amen*

Reflection:

Prayer:

Regardless

DAY 16

Remember

"Oh, that we were back in Egypt," they moaned. "It would have been better if the Lord had killed us there! At least there we had plenty to eat. But now, you have brought us into this desert to starve us to death."

Exodus 16:3 (NLT)

The children of Israel were freed from captivity, walked on the dried surface of the Red Sea, saw their enemies being "swept into raging currents" (Exodus 14:27), and sang songs of deliverance to the Lord. And now, a month into their journey to The Promised Land, they raised their entitled voices to complain about their perceived conditions and, in their delirium, preferred to die or return to their former state.

It's so easy to lift our voices in thanksgiving when things are going well. However, a true sign of spiritual enlightenment is the ability to see God in the midst of our circumstances, to remember His track record in our lives, and to give Him praise despite how we feel. After all, feelings always change, but God is completely reliable.

It really doesn't matter what we're facing, our circumstances have not caught God by surprise. In fact, He frequently allows our way to become uncomfortable so that we recognize our need for Him. We are admonished to take our eyes off our situations and look to Him *Regardless*. He's aware of our needs, hears our prayers, and is working on our behalf.

Remember that He's a good, compassionate and forward-thinking God. He knows what we need and has our provision.

Prayer

We are so grateful that you are so good. We've seen you come to our rescue, bring us out of impossible situations, and open so many doors. Thank you for being God.

In Jesus' Name,

Amen

Reflection:

Prayer:

DAY 17

Rely

"For I know the plans I have for you," says the Lord. "They are plans for good and not for disaster, to give you a future and a hope. In those days when you pray, I will listen. If you look for me in earnest, you will find me when you seek me ...."

Jeremiah 29:11-12 (NLT)

Our lives were not created to be a haphazard set of circumstances. We were created intentionally. Our difficulties and our delights have purpose when our goal is to honor Him despite what we're feeling. After all, feelings are circumstantial and unreliable. They can't be depended upon to reveal the truths of a situation.

When we choose to rely on Christ as our Source, we have certain guarantees:

- First, He knows us. The God of all creation is the Architect of our lives. He's intricately aware of how we think and feel and knows our every inclination. We can ask Him to direct us and tell us what we need to know.

- Second, He sees us and is with us. We may have our individual thoughts and experience a myriad of emotions, but He's with us in and through them all. We're not alone. We can choose to recognize His presence and seek His comfort.

- Third, He has plans for each of us. Every circumstance in life has meaning to Him. Every tear that falls from our faces can water a garden of promise. He can take the pain, struggle, and triumphs we experience and orchestrate outcomes that will leave us speechless.

God attends to the affairs of the world while simultaneously focusing on our individual needs. He allows joy and pain to enter our lives and uses these events to draw our attention to Him and to remind us to depend on Him. We can trust and rely on God who is present, loving, and intentional.

Prayer

Your thoughts about us are good, and your plans for us are perfect. Thank you, Lord, for being an ever-present God who invites us to depend on you.

In Jesus' Name,

Amen

Reflection:

Prayer:

DAY 18

Good God!

The Lord Almighty is among us; the God of Israel is our fortress.

Psalm 46:11 (NIV)

Trustworthy God. Our God has proven His commitment to us. He has demonstrated His love and care, holding back the hand of evil and showing up when we call. He gives the assurance we need and waits for our response.

Gracious God. God has been with us all along, tending to the affairs of our lives. We are living testimonies of His presence and benefactors of His favor. We have received more than we deserve and exist under the canopy of His kindness every day.

Present God. We were born into circumstances we did not craft, grew in homes we did not buy, and lived with people we did not choose. Loved ones have ignored our needs and friends have walked away, but the Lord of hosts has been with us (Psalm 46:7) and has never abandoned us.

Preserving God. When our minds have contemplated the unthinkable and our hearts have felt as though they could literally break, we've been comforted, encouraged, and strengthened to continue the course for one more day. Difficult decisions have been made and opportunities have been taken away, but He has kept us in perfect peace

(Isaiah 26:3). He has committed to securing our well-being as we've committed to following His course.

Protective God. Every dawn and every dusk have exposed the safety and security of His hand. God has been our refuge, our hiding place. We've matured and faced the realities of life, received insulation from the consequences of poor decision-making, and have been given what we've needed to face our difficulties. He has protected without our knowledge and has provided comfort when fears shatter our peace.

Good God. Who else has lavished us with the gifts of life and forgiveness? He has blessed us beyond our imaginations, freely giving of His lovingkindness and tender mercies to those too naïve to truly comprehend. Our God has given us the advantage to know Him, to serve Him, and to love Him.

Deserving God. Now the choice for us is clear: give Him our pittance or give Him our all? Show up to live well or be present on our own terms? A God who has been as He is deserves the best of who we are. He is great so that we can be and do good.

Prayer

Lord, thank you for being our good and gracious God. Teach us how to demonstrate your kindness to others as our act of gratitude to You.

In Jesus' Name,

Amen

Reflection:

Prayer:

Regardless

DAY 19

Boast!

But He said, "My grace is sufficient for you, for power is perfect in weakness." Therefore, I will most gladly boast all the more about my weaknesses, so that Christ's power may reside in me.

2 Corinthians 12:9 (NLT)

Christ offers more. Yes, His grace is unmerited; we need it every moment of every day, but his grace is also strength. We can be weak by the standards that society sets and yet strong in our thoughts, emotions, and daily living. We can choose personal weakness that empowers us to press forward despite all that tries to pull us back and break us down.

Christ's grace has effect--it is enough. We don't need to search for answers in fickle places. The strength of Christ becomes evident when our help arrives, when we can do "it" one more time, when we can pray for "her" despite the way she's treated us, when we can help "them" even when we're tired, and when we can leave "that" alone because it's the better choice. Grace can carry us through, shelter us, and protect us *Regardless* of what we face.

We, ourselves, are insufficient. He is Shaddai, Sufficient. His is our strength, gives us our strength, and renews our strength. We can boast of His goodness, greatness, and grace. Because He is who He is and does what He does, we can say:

"He has everything I need!"
"He always shows up when I need Him!"
"He's worthy to be praised!"

Prayer

Lord, we are feeble and hopeless without your grace. We want to honor You and reflect your goodness. And when you bring our resolutions, we want others to see that it had nothing to do with us and everything to do with You. Thank you for your grace.

In Jesus' Name,

Amen

Reflection:

Prayer:

DAY 20

Blessed

You prepare a feast for me in the presence of my enemies. You welcome me as a guest, anointing my head with oil. My cup overflows with blessing.

Psalm 23:5 (NLT)

We are indeed blessed to have food, clothing, shelter, and our ample portion of health and strength. But when we enthusiastically say, "I'm blessed!" are we narrowly referring to what we give or receive? Are we living at the surface of our faith or willingly acknowledging and embracing the deeper definition of what it means to be a Christian?

The beginning of Psalm 23 reveals everything. Verse 1 says, "The Lord is my Shepherd." That's a declaration of the nature of God and His relationship with us. It speaks to the connection, inter-relatedness, and agreement between God and His people. He's not just a supplier of things and opportunities. He covers and protects those who are His own. He leads so that we can follow and will direct us to sustenance and refreshment for our journey. He takes his guardianship role seriously. He will give us what is needed at the very moment it is needed. God will provide.

Regardless of our daily realities, we are beneficiaries of fortunate circumstances because we are children of God. Our lives have the potential to be gifts to others, and we have the opportunity to benefit from choosing to live a life of obedience.

The truth about being blessed is that we have the privilege of building an intimate relationship with our Father, the Good Shepherd. But we have to give ourselves to the relationship so that our commitment drives our access. It's not about having an advantage or being lucky. A rabbit's foot can't change our lives and a four leaf clover can't provide covering. What we have is kinship—the tie that binds and never bends or breaks.

He is the God who dries our tears and sends our help. Only this God provides a spiritual reservoir that feeds our emotional needs. We are blessed to overflowing because we've accepted Him as our Lord.

We can look forward to a future of promise with the assurance of experience. He has blessed us with His presence. He has welcomed us into His fold. He has given in great measure with a promise that never ends. We are blessed because He is good.

Prayer

Lord, you are indeed good. Thank you for the privilege of calling you our Good Shepherd and for the gift of relationship. You have blessed us with your presence, guidance, provision, and protection, and we are deeply grateful. We want to make a daily, conscious decision to pursue relationship with you.

In Jesus' Name,

Amen

Regardless

Reflection:

Prayer:

DAY 21

Bless Him

Bless the Lord, O my soul: and all that is within me, bless his holy name. Bless the Lord, O my soul, and forget not all his benefits...

Psalm 103: 1-2 (KJV)

Sometimes all we can say is "Thank you, Lord", but at other times it's a shortcut. Our gracious, giving God deserves to hear us express our admiration and gratitude and be specific about what we've seen, heard, and experienced. He wants us to be vocal about who He is and what He has done so that our hearts have the opportunity to swell with thanksgiving as an alternative expression to world events, irrational thinking, and personal choices.

There's a lot of ruckus all around us and we need to focus on what's true. God has been good, and we need to tell Him what we've noticed. He healed us even when we we're certain that He would. God has provided what we've needed in what felt like the last minute, but we now know was right on time. He encouraged us to be quiet and listen when we could have blown it with our words. God has been forgiving and giving and kind. He has been our Provider, Encourager, and Friend. We have homes, jobs and churches, family members and friends. We think back on the kinds of decisions we've made and recognize God's graciousness. We don't deserve what He has given, and for that alone, He deserves our time, attention, and praise.

Blessing God simply means that we take the time to recognize Him as our Source for everything. It's the opportunity we have to celebrate who He is and shower Him with our words, thoughts, and praise. It's all about Him. We bless Him when we tell Him that we see Him doing things around us, sense Him speaking to us, and are grateful for who He is. We can tell him, "God, you are good", "Thank you, Lord", "Bless the Lord", or any other words that help to frame our awe and appreciation for our King of Kings. He is greater than any other and does all things well, so let's bless Him.

Prayer

Lord, thank you for life, health, and strength, in whatever measure we're given. Thank you for the coins in our purse and for being with us as we travel to and fro. For providing more than we need, we give you thanks. For protecting us from what escapes us, we are grateful. Our circumstances aren't perfect, but you're developing hearts of contentment and appreciation by opening our eyes to your graciousness. You remain at work on our behalf.

Lord, these words come from meager lips to lift praise and thanks to you in recognition of your kindness and faithfulness. Our hearts are glad because you are our God. When we stop to think of all that You have done that we are aware of, and then consider all that you do that we have no knowledge of or appreciation for, we are overcome with thanks and praise. You are worthy to be praised. From sunrise to sunset, we will lift our eyes to Heaven and say, "Bless the Lord, O my soul and all that is within me, bless His holy name." The more we repeat these verses, the more we realize that you are our sufficiency and our lives lack meaning outside of your will.

Thank you for giving us the words to say. We can use these verses as our prayer throughout the day, "Bless the Lord, O my soul ...."

In Jesus' Name,

Amen

Reflection:

Prayer:

DAY 22

Access

God is our refuge and strength, always ready to help in times of trouble.

Psalm 46:1 (NLT)

The issue is not whether God is present, but whether we believe that He's present for us. It's so easy to encourage others to trust Him and believe that He will open doors and provide recovery and protection. But when the issue is at our own address, and it's our turn to make His promises personal, we stutter and shake, doubt and avoid.

The truth we share is the truth we must embrace. Yes, He is accessible to our girlfriends and sisters. And yes, He is available and willing to act for us, too. He wants to demonstrate His strength and be realized in every part of our lives, including our unrelenting circumstances. He is a personal God and wants to demonstrate personally His love and regard for us.

The King James Version of Psalm 46:1 says that He is "a very present help". That denotes a steady presence and fixed position. Since He doesn't move, He can be accessed at any time. Our Loving Father is attainable, consistent, and able to be all that we need *Regardless* of the calamities we face. He is our very own hiding place, our personal security, our secret shelter, our relief, and our source of strength. He has what we need at the very moment we need it. Call Him. Ask Him. Seek Him. Embrace Him. Access Him.

Prayer

 Lord, thank you for being a prayer away. When we can't depend on ourselves or anyone else, we can always depend on You. When our social networks fail and personal relationships change, You remain the same. We are grateful for full access to You.

     In Jesus' Name,

     Amen

Reflection:

Prayer:

DAY 23

Consecrate

Yours, O Lord is the greatness, the power, the glory, the victory, and the majesty. Everything in the heavens and on earth is yours, O Lord, and this is your kingdom. We adore you as the one who is over all things.

1 Chronicles 29:11 (NLT)

Anything that we decide to give back to the Lord was already His from the beginning. We have nothing to give until He gives first. We can't give our lives until He gives life. We don't have funds until He supplies them; and if we become forgetful, He can choose to remove what He's given to us or remove us from them.

Since all we have is His, our personal consecration is an appropriate response to His grace. We can consecrate or dedicate what we 'have' to remind ourselves of our unworthiness and His absolute worthiness. We, then, set our passions on putting material things in their fickle place. After all, anything we can possess can collect dust, mold, and rust. But when our hearts are set to return to Him what He has given, we possess those things without being possessed by them.

We consecrate as an act of prayer. It's our opportunity to say, "Thank you, Lord, for trusting me with this. Now, please teach me how to use it to bless someone and honor You." It's a choice we make not to be known for our possessions, but to be known as the possessed. It is the richest, most rewarding kind of possession where we recognize that we are His to be used as He desires and all that we have is given for greater purpose.

Prayer of Consecration

    Lord, you own it all. Use what you have given us to help, heal, and bring hope to others while glorifying yourself.

In Jesus' Name,

Amen

Reflection:

Prayer:

DAY 24

Don't Worry

Don't worry about anything ....

Philippians 4:6a (NLT)

Worry has a purpose. It can occupy our minds, rev up our emotions, and lead us to consider irrational ideas. The stress associated with worrying can decrease the function of vital organs and can reduce our ability to think and communicate clearly. It slows us down and curtails our effectiveness.

When we decide to worry, we invite a separation between our minds, emotions and actions and God's perfect intentions for us. We become busy rehearsing the "maybe's" and "what if's" that lead to distorted perspectives and personal torment. When we make worry a practice, our anxieties grow, and our peace of mind becomes disturbed. So, worrying has purpose, but it's not beneficial.

The most effective impact of worrying is that our minds are taught to avoid, minimize, and disbelieve what is real, true, and dependable. The truth is that prayer really does bring about change. We can tell God about everything that concerns us, and He listens and responds. So, whether we need a parking space or next month's mortgage, we can tell Him about it, ask Him for what we need, and thank Him for how He will respond.

Practicing gratitude reminds us of His faithfulness, and, in return, we experience an emotional lift and renewed perspective. When we choose to look to God in the midst of our circumstances, He will provide the peace that will keep us, encourage us, and strengthen us *Regardless* of what's happening.

Today, we can experience the relief of resting on our strong-armed Savior. We can actively participate in combating our concerns and anxieties with courage, gratitude and the truth. How?

- *Talk about it.* Be honest about the issues that are scary, hurtful, or we'd prefer to avoid. God already knows of what we're afraid. He knows what keeps us up at night and what preoccupies our minds. To live in the truth, we need to name the issues that plague us before we can learn to rest in His promises.

- *Demonstrate gratitude.* The Bible says, "No matter what happens, always be thankful, for this is God's will for you who belong to Christ Jesus" (1 Thessalonians 5:18). God has infused significant benefits into living a thankful life. Our outlook improves, and we're always more pleasant to be around when we have a grateful heart.

- *Pray frequently.* 1 Thessalonians 5:17 tells us to "Keep on praying". In other words, develop the kind of mindset and lifestyle that maintains constant communication with God. In return, we gain clarity of thought and direction, and we're less likely to let our difficulties control our actions.

- *Change the focus.* Develop a singular focus and begin to listen to the truth that can be found at the level of the heart. Ask God for direction and expect Him to respond. Avoid making comparisons or excuses; instead, expect change and work toward it.

Prayer

Lord, worrying is a lot of work with disturbing results. Today, help us to look to You, rely on You, and accept the peace that only comes from You.

In Jesus' Name,

Amen

Reflection:

Prayer:

DAY 25

Give Thanks

The Lord is my strength, my shield from every danger. I trust in him with all my heart. He helps me, and my heart is filled with joy. I burst out in songs of thanksgiving.

Psalm 28:7 (NLT)

It takes less than a minute for a yielded heart to recognize how good God is. Whether today or ten years ago, He has demonstrated His love and compassion to us. Take the time to think about what He has done over the course of the last month. Has He not been good? Despite and because of all that we deal with, He has made himself known in every situation. In illness, He has been our strength. In calamity, He has provided relief. In grief and despair, He has comforted us.

The harvest of food on a holiday table can't begin to demonstrate the depth of gratitude that comes from a heart that notices God's handiwork. He has been good! Our life circumstances are as they are because He is who He is. God has provided for us in ways that we are still unaware. He has opened and closed doors of opportunity because He always has His glory and our best interest in mind. He protects, provides, and empowers. He listens, and speaks, and reminds. He is an ever-present God who neither leaves us nor forsakes us (Deuteronomy 31:6) and has everything we need. He is our sufficiency (2 Peter 1:3).

Don Moen is often credited with singing the song "Give Thanks" that was written by Henry Smith (1978). Mr. Smith penned the words while facing financial and health challenges. He recognized God's goodness despite his personal challenges and shared his insight with the world:

> Give thanks with a grateful heart
> Give thanks to the Holy One
> Give thanks because He's given Jesus Christ, His Son
> And now let the weak say, "I am strong"
> Let the poor say, "I am rich
> Because of what the Lord has done for us"
> Give thanks.

Prayer

Thank you, Lord for being the Presence that meets our needs in every situation. Time and time again you have proven your love and care for us, and we are filled with gratitude.

In Jesus' Name,

Amen

Reflection:

Prayer:

Regardless

DAY 26

Imagine

So, we don't look at the troubles we see right now; rather, we look forward to what we have not seen. For troubles we see will soon be over, but the joys to come will last forever.

2 Corinthians 4:18 (NLT)

Troubles often skew our view, narrow our perspective, and limit the way we think about God. If we're willing to exhibit child-like faith, we will look beyond our circumstances to see His promises. This thing we're facing is temporary. We're not alone or without hope or help; the timer on our issue is running out.

> *Dear brothers and sisters, whenever trouble comes your way,*
> *let it be an opportunity for joy. for when your faith is tested,*
> *your endurance has a chance to grow.*
> *James 1:2-3*

When we're emotionally invested in our circumstances, we can't always envision what's ahead of us. By choosing to release our limited point-of-view, we are free to demonstrate the kind of faith that allows us to see things from God's panoramic position. Then our imagination can line up with His plan and our posture will be slanted toward a spiritual perspective.

The hopes of the godly result in happiness, but the
expectations of the wicked are in vain.

Proverbs 10:28

There's more to life than the issues we face. There's more to look forward to than our present circumstance. We each have a big, bright, beautiful future on the horizon. Life's distractions and distresses cause us to forget to grab hold of the certainty that is ours; we will have joy that will not end. Imagine that!

Prayer

Lord, thank you for the gift of perspective that allows us to see things as You see them. Because we know that you are with us and that you have a plan for us, we also know that the best is yet to come.

In Jesus' Name,

Amen

Reflection:

Prayer:

DAY 27

In His Hands

For the life of every living thing is in his hand, and the breath of all humanity.

Job 12: 10 (NLT)

Success or failure, joy or pain, health or sickness, blessings or calamity, God controls it all. God is not just God when things are going well. He's God *Regardless* of what's happening.

It's easy to forget that He has a front row seat to our life's circumstances. God has provided permissions for all our experiences. He's intimately aware. When we pray for that new position or opportunity, He opens or shuts doors. When we seek Him for healing, He restores now, later, or never. When we're uncertain about what to do, He confirms, directs, burdens, or warns.

God looks down and in and through all situations. He has the inside track. God not only gives the gift of life, but He provides the direction for the gift and manages its welfare. That's the lesson that Job knew well. In the face of doubting friends, He would remain confident that God's decisions were right for his life. His losses would somehow lead to gain. Job knew that everything was in God's hand.

We can take heart and be encouraged. God is on the job and is not asleep. Whether for our spouses or children, parents or friends, bosses or employees, leaders or neighbors, they are in His hands. In our bedroom or workroom, right now or in five days, we are in His hands.

Prayer

   Dear Father, thank you for taking such good care of us. Teach us to surrender to your will and follow your leadings.

In Jesus' Name,

Amen

Reflection:

Prayer:

DAY 28

Recognize

I am the one who creates the light and makes the darkness. I am the one who sends good times and bad times, I the Lord am the one who does these things.

Isaiah 45:7 (NLT)

How often do we need to be reminded that we have no control over anything? We have no ability and possess no skill without God's decision. He brings to us good and bad experiences as a mark of His wisdom. He teaches us to be thankful despite our circumstances and to look to Him for everything we need.

God demonstrates His greatness in the lives of His people. He's not shy to show us who He is and to give us a glimpse of His glory. We can easily recognize the unexplainable when babies are born, when an impaired elder regains the ability to walk, when a deaf person and a hearing person engage in conversation, and when children develop the ability to express themselves using gestures and strings of words.

Today, we can we see the demonstration of His faithfulness in our ordinary lives and give Him thanks. He's in control and won't abandon or forget our needs. He is without rival and deserves our recognition.

Prayer

Lord, thank you for doing things that we can't explain and causing us to remember that You control everything.

In Jesus' Name,

Amen

Reflection:

Prayer:

Regardless

DAY 29

Follow

Jesus said to the people, "I am the light of the world. If you follow me, you won't be stumbling through the darkness, because you will have the light that leads to life."

John 8:12 (NLT)

It can be both scary and annoying to search for something or search for some clear path, without a source of light. There's a constant concern that you'll bump your toe on a chair leg, or on another object before you find what you're looking for or reach your destination. Whether by power outage or your own will, you find yourself searching, fumbling, and hoping. Without light, you just might hurt yourself. A phone light, flashlight, or lamp would make your task more manageable and safer.

Light illuminates—exposing what can't be seen in the dark. It provides security. To be realized, it needs to be reflected. Christ allows our hearts to detect and reflect His light. Its origin is radiant and provides a broad scope for those who are equipped to perceive it.

Following Christ means always having the illuminant available to bring clarity and direction. Our task is to look to, then follow the Light. We're not to walk ahead of it or presume its direction but should rather step-by-step, moment-by-moment, allow ourselves to be guided. And, when we have vision, we can live our lives with focus, direction, and impact.

Prayer

Lord, thank you that we have no need to be clueless. You make us aware of everything we need to know. Teach us to look for you when we can't think clearly, when we're confused about the best decisions to make, and when we're afraid. We can be certain that You will provide direction.

In Jesus' Name,

Amen

Reflection:

Prayer:

DAY 30

Go!

Be strong and courageous! Do not be afraid of them! The Lord your God will go ahead of you. He will neither fail you nor forsake you.

Deuteronomy 31:6 (NLT)

The time had come for Moses to retire from his work. Now Joshua would lead. The mission did not change. The people of Israel were to cross the Jordan River into the Promised Land, but they'd do this with a new leader. Moses admonished them not to be intimidated by what was to come. God had prepared the way and would be with them. In fact, God promised to destroy the enemies that were currently living in their land. The same God who had protected them and provided a dry escape from Egypt would now be with the people as they crossed over into new territory. He would provide a complete victory though some of their enemies were giant and fierce. With these encouragements, Moses was teaching the people to depend on God.

Every day that we place our feet on the rug beside our beds, we should give thanks for the day, and then remind ourselves that despite the challenges we may face, God has gone before us and is with us. We can "walk by faith" (2 Corinthians 5:7) knowing that God is aware of the terrain. Our Loving Father will clear a path for us even when the course seems long, with unyielding curves. His presence and assurances will provide us with the courage we need to continue our journey.

There are new territories to be realized, new opportunities to pursue, new people to impact, and some change to take place in our day — today. We must pray and face each detail that confronts us. As we press forward, we go with God.

Prayer

Lord, thank you for not only being a consistent presence but for paving the way for us and for helping us to navigate the rough terrain in our lives. What's before us can seem so challenging at times. Thank you for being the kind of God who encourages, directs, provides, and supports so that we can press forward . . .

.

In Jesus' Name,

Amen

Reflection:

Prayer:

Regardless

DAY 31

Wait and ....

I say to myself, "The Lord is my inheritance; therefore, I will hope in him!" The Lord is wonderfully good to those who wait for him and seek him. So, it is good to wait quietly for salvation from the Lord.

Lamentations 3: 24-26 (NLT)

Christ is our Progenitor. He gives us direction, serves as our model, passes on his characteristics to us, and provides our sufficient portion. He is our inheritance. And He promises to be good to us if we wait on Him *and* seek Him.

We're not asked to look up for manna from heaven to drop down for us. Doing nothing until we get His answer or direction is not the productive response. It's certainly not in our best interest to act first and ask questions later. That can lead to disaster. Even when we experience emergent situations we can choose to pray and then act. We are called to imitate His character-to do what He has shown us to do.

As we walk through our circumstances, we can ask Him what He wants us to do, then actively wait until we sense His response or see His purposes revealed. We can busy ourselves with doing what we frequently try to avoid: praying, meditating, studying His Word, and developing a surrendered attitude.

When we "wait quietly" we wait without complaint. We learn to be thankful that things are as they are and recognize our need for Him and the salvation He brings. In so doing, we demonstrate our trust and reliance on Him. He will respond with everything we need and will decide when to answer our call.

Prayer

Father in Heaven, we have the assurance that You know us and hear us. We will wait for your response even when waiting is uncomfortable. Thank you for being the God we can trust.

In Jesus' Name,

Amen

Reflection:

Prayer:

Regardless

References

Hall, D. (1980). Ordinary People. Universal Music-MGB Songs, Birdwing Music & Sandtree Music. Retrieved from: https://www.musicnotes.com/sheetmusic/mtd.asp?ppn=MN0076651

Life Application Study Bible: New Living Translation (1996). Wheaton, Il: Tyndale House Publishers.

Tindley, C.A. (1905). Storm is passing over. *Soul Echos*. United States of America. Retrieved from: http://www.hymntime.com/tch/bio/t/i/n/tindley_ca.htm

Smith, H. (1978). Give Thanks. United States of America. Retrieved from: https://hymnary.org/tune/give_thanks_smith

Regardless

Regardless

Regardless

Regardless

Made in the USA
Coppell, TX
07 December 2020